THE *Wonder* OF IT ALL

A DEVOTIONAL BOOK
to exemplify the beauty of the Creator's works and to encourage all of us to walk in His ways

The Wonder of It All

There's the wonder of sunset at evening,
The wonder as sunrise I see;
But the wonder of wonders that thrills my soul
Is the wonder that God loves me.

There's the wonder of springtime and harvest,
The sky, the stars, the sun;
But the wonder of wonders that thrills my soul
Is the wonder that's only begun.

O, the wonder of it all! The wonder of it all!
Just to think that God loves me.

THE WONDER OF *G*OD AROUND US

THE WONDER OF *G*OD FOR US

THE WONDER OF *G*OD WITH US

ℱOREWORD

In 1955, the Billy Graham team traveled to Scotland for a month of crusades. On the journey there, I met with a gentleman who was a New York music publisher. He knew of my privileged connection with the Billy Graham Evangelistic Association, and we talked about this. And, too, I learned a little more about the music world. Although he was a man of another faith, we found that we had an abiding interest in hymns, gospel music, and the great classics as played by the world's finest orchestras.

But I was glad when our conversation turned back to the Billy Graham ministry. For suddenly he asked, "What goes on in these huge gatherings at Mr. Graham's missions?" Not having the eloquence of a Billy Graham or Cliff Barrows, I simply began to speak of the large volunteer choirs and the tender preaching of the Word expressed with such warmth by the voice of the gracious Southern gentleman, Billy Graham. Too soon, however, I seemed to run out of words and exclaimed, "Oh, sir, if you could just see it—the wonder of it all!" He quickly pulled an envelope from his pocket, wrote those very words, and said, "I commission you to write a song with this title."

Later, upon witnessing a magnificent sunset, I began to pen the words and music, giving thankful expression to our loving God for all His wonders. And that was the beginning of a new song that would be sung to hearts everywhere, inviting people to gaze on God's glorious creation and pause long enough "just to think that God loves me."

When you look at God's creation through Tom Fox's photographs, you'll get just a glimpse of the wonder of God's glory. But what a glimpse of glory it is! How marvelous to see God's creative beauty displayed in the water's reflection, the majesty of the mountains at sunrise, the stillness of the moon at nightfall!

And what a blessing to read Adrian Rogers' devotional thoughts alongside these remarkable images of God's creation. My spirit was refreshed and encouraged as I read Dr. Rogers' poignant thoughts from God's Word, His unique way of describing the wonders of God's great gifts to us all.

Oh, the wonder of it all! Truly it is hard to put into words the joy that wells up in my heart as I receive spiritual uplift from every page of this fine book, named after the song that came to my heart so long ago. I know this book will become a favorite of yours, as it has of mine.

George Beverly Shea

THE WONDER

OF *God*

AROUND US

THE WONDER OF GOD AROUND US

GOD'S SOVEREIGNTY IN CREATION

I am the maker of all things.

ISAIAH 44:24

God made all things. Every person you see. Every blade of grass. Every grain of sand. Every star that glistens in the night sky. God made them all. We simply cannot escape the awesome wonder of God in this world. It's impossible. His thumbprint is on everything. And the same God Who created all things makes salvation possible through His Son Jesus Christ and makes sanctification possible through the indwelling of His Holy Spirit. Praise God for His wonder around us!

IN THE *Beginning*

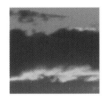

In the beginning God created the heavens and the earth.
Then God said, "Let there be light."

You and I will never exhaust the profound truths in the first verse of Genesis as we bring our little teacup minds to this great ocean of truth. In fact, we will never truly comprehend anything else in the Bible unless we understand Genesis 1:1. The key to the rest of the Bible is hung right here on the front door of God's Word. Man cannot create. Only God can create. The only way you will understand God's awesome power in creation is by faith. Hebrews 11:3 tells us, *"Through faith we understand that the worlds were framed by the word of God, so that things which are seen were not made of things which do appear."* All creation speaks of the presence of God. Oh, the mighty, mighty power of God. The entire universe has a stamp on it that reads, "MADE BY GOD."

WIND RIVER RANGE, WYOMING

OF *Water* AND SPIRIT

And the Spirit of God was moving

over the surface of the waters.

GENESIS 1:2

First Peter 4:19 speaks of God as a "faithful Creator." Did God make this world, then wind it up, fling it out into space, and turn His back on it? No. He Who made this world will care for it. Isaiah 43:2-3 is a beautiful picture of His loving care: "*...when thou passeth through the waters, I will be with thee; and through the rivers, they shall not overflow thee...For I am the* LORD *thy God, the Holy One of Israel.*" God is saying, "I made you, I will save you, and I will stay with you." God is a powerful, personal, purposeful God. He made you for a purpose, and He has promised to watch over you.

ZION NATIONAL PARK, UTAH

ORDER IN *NATURE*

I, the LORD, am the maker of all things.

ISAIAH 44:24

Everything we see has been perfectly designed by the Master Creator. Our universe was created in absolute and supreme order. Night follows day, and day follows night—all because God placed our planet in perfectly synchronized, orbital revolutions. Aristotle said, *"The beauty, the order, and the harmony of the universe is but an expression of the will of God."* When you look at a watch, you assume there's a watchmaker. The intricate precision with which a watch is made demands that there is a maker behind it—a maker, but not a creator. Men can't create anything. Man makes a watch to record the time that God has created. There is only one Creator, and He is Jehovah. Glory to God that every atom is perfectly created for our survival. Oh, the wonder of it all!

CAPITOL REEF NATIONAL PARK, UTAH

HEAVEN'S *DECLARATION*

*The heavens declare the glory of God;
the skies proclaim the work of his hands.*

PSALM 19:1

I don't know when David wrote Psalm 19, but I can imagine what he might have been thinking about when he wrote about the heavens declaring the glory of God. Maybe he remembered when he was a little shepherd boy lying flat on his back looking up into the starry Judean sky. Perhaps he recalled seeing the moon and the stars against the black velvet of heaven when he was a king on the battlefield. Wherever he was, he was on target. Indeed, all of creation declares the glory of God! The trees sway in the breeze as if to resonate a praise to the Lord. The flowers joyfully lift their petals in praise. The birds sing praises. The mighty oceans heave their billows and shout, "PRAISE GOD!" The lofty mountains peer through the clouds at One higher than they. The Niagara cascades mighty praises to the Great Creator. And you, too, were made to praise Him. Rejoice! He has made His glory known to all of creation!

La Sal Mountains, Utah

AFTER THEIR *KIND*

Then God said, "Let the earth bring forth
living creatures after their kind."

GENESIS 1:24

Do you want a three-word argument against evolution? "After their kind." God made every creature unique. There is no evolution of the species; each were created "after their kind." Let me tell you four things the evolutionist cannot explain. First, the origin of life. How does life come from non-life? Second, the fixity of the species. Why do we have mutation within a species, but never transmutation? Third, the Second Law of Thermodynamics—everything is subject to death, decay, and disintegration. Can time plus chance turn frogs into princes? Fourth, the nonphysical properties found in creation. Where do music, art, and an innate hunger for God originate? The creative majesty of this world is a glorious mystery that we will never fully understand. But, that's okay. We serve a great God Who does.

YELLOWSTONE NATIONAL PARK, WYOMING

IN HIS *Image*

And God created man in His own image.

GENESIS 1:27

Is mankind simply the result of a chain of chromosomes which evolved into an eternal soul of higher intelligence and moral conviction? Some would like us to think that. But let me say on the authority of the Word of God that man did not evolve; he was uniquely and divinely created in the image of God. What does that mean? I believe the image of God refers to God's spiritual attributes rather than His physical attributes. Colossians 3:10 and Ephesians 4:24 tell us that the "new man" is made after the image of God Who is perfect holiness, absolute love, and supreme knowledge. *"I will praise thee; for I am fearfully and wonderfully made: marvelous are thy works; and that my soul knoweth right well."* (Psalm 139:14). Thank God for the way He has lovingly created every ounce and every inch of who you are. And thank Him for His power that sustains your next heartbeat!

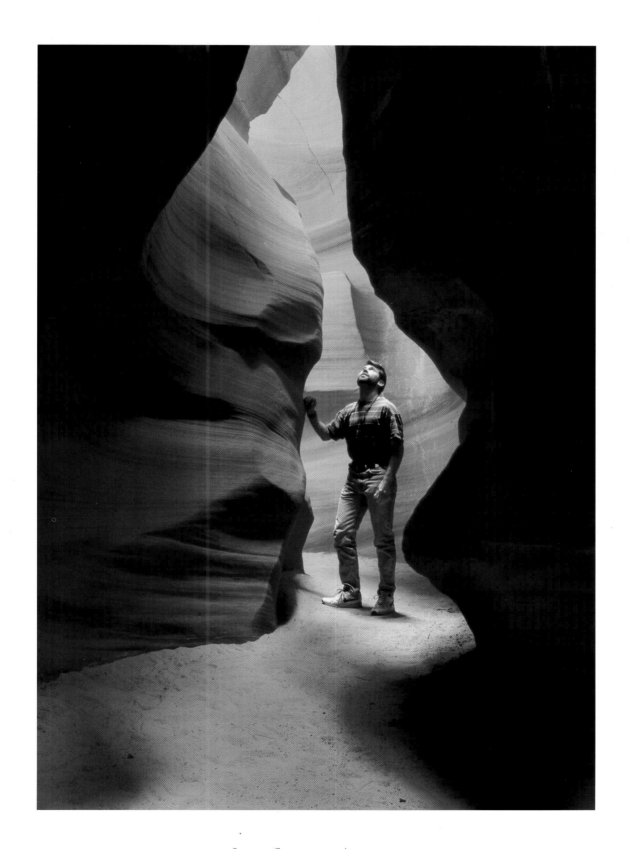

SLOT CANYON, ARIZONA

A PLACE CALLED *E*DEN

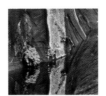

*T*hen the L<small>ORD</small> *God took the man*

and put him into the garden of Eden to cultvate it and keep it.

<small>GENESIS</small> 2:15

God created man to rule over His creation—to *"cultivate it and keep it"* (Genesis 2:15, NASB). God gave him dominion to work the earth and to protect and guard its inhabitants (see Genesis 1:26-28; 9:2-3). From the beginning of time, man was given the divine responsibility to care for God's created world. Psalm 8:5-8 tells us that God *"made him a little lower than the heavenly beings and crowned him with glory and honor. You [God] made him ruler over the works of your hands; you put everything under his feet: all flocks and herds, and the beasts of the field, the birds of the air, and the fish of the sea, all that swim the paths of the seas"* (NIV). The glorious riches of this land are ours to enjoy and to keep. What a momentous, yet humbling task God has given each of us!

ESCALANTE WILDERNESS AREA, UTAH

THE TREE OF *Life*

And the LORD *God planted a garden . . .*
[with] the tree of life also in the midst of the garden.

GENESIS 2:8,9

In the midst of the Garden of Eden, God omnisciently planted two trees—a tree of life and a tree of "death." The tree of death refers to the "tree of knowledge of good and evil" from which Adam and Eve ate. The other tree—the tree of life—symbolizes the tree upon which our Lord Jesus died to give us everlasting life (see Revelation 2:7). The first Adam ate of the tree of knowledge and was driven from paradise. A thief hanging on a cross next to Jesus "ate" of the second tree and was invited into paradise (see Luke 23:39-43). In the words of one of my favorite hymns, *"His sacrifice on Calvary has made the mighty cross a tree of life for me."* Oh, the mighty love of Jesus—the love that would stop at nothing, not even death, to save us!

Slot Canyon, Arizona

MAJESTY

Thine, O LORD, is the greatness and the power
and the glory and the victory and the majesty.

I CHRONICLES 29:11

Anything you make must be manufactured from something else, right? Not so with God. God created everything out of nothing. John 1:3 says, *"All things were made by him; and without him was not any thing made that was made."* Only by faith can you ever understand this miraculous truth. God spoke, and it was so. I like what an eloquent preacher had to say about creation. He said, *"God stepped from behind the curtain of nowhere, stood on the platform of nothing, and spoke a universe into existence."* Look at the majestic beauty of this mountain in the Grand Tetons National Park. Can you even comprehend the Almighty power of God? He said it was so, and it was!

GRAND TETONS NATIONAL PARK, WYOMING

*W*ONDERS

*G*reat are the works of the LORD . . .

He has made His wonders to be remembered.

PSALM 111:2,4

Years ago, I read about an argument between some of Napoleon's soldiers concerning the existence of God. Napoleon pointed to the stars and said, *"Gentlemen, before you deny the fact of God, you'll have to get rid of those."* The wonder of God's creation nullifies man's reasoning for not believing in the existence of an Almighty, Divine Creator. Romans 1:20 says, *"For the invisible things of him from the creation of the world are clearly seen, being understood by the things that are made, even his eternal power and Godhead; so that they are without excuse."* Indeed, we cannot fathom the depth and breadth of His divine creativity. Great are the works of God!

GRAND CANYON NATIONAL PARK, ARIZONA

CIRQUE OF THE *Towers*

I will lift up my eyes to the mountains;

from whence shall my help come?

My help comes from the LORD, *who made heaven and earth.*

PSALM 121:1-2

One of the grandest statements I ever read about God's wonderful creation and His ever-present care came from a fellow evangelist, Angel Martinez. He said, *"The Lord, the One who made the world and everything that is in it, the One who lit the taper of the sun and put the stars in their places, that's my Shepherd. The One who threw a carpet of green grass upon the earth and tacked it down with flowers, the One who scooped up the valleys and piled up the hills, the One who took the song of the seraph and robed it with feathers and gave it to the nightingale, the One who took the rainbow and wove it into a scarf and threw it about the shoulders of a dying storm, that's my Shepherd. At evening time, He pulls down the shade of the night and shoots it through with sunset fire."* The Lord, who created all things, will help you. He is your Shepherd who is ever-watching and ever-loving.

WIND RIVER RANGE, WYOMING

FROM *E*VERLASTING TO EVERLASTING

*B*efore the mountains were born,

or Thou didst give birth to the earth and the world,

even from everlasting to everlasting, Thou art God.

PSALM 90:2

What does it mean that something is everlasting? I think the evangelist, Billy Sunday, explained it best. He said, *"Imagine a little bird taking a grain of sand from the earth and flying for a million years to a distant planet. When he reaches the planet, he drops that grain of sand. He makes the return trip of a million years to earth to get another grain of sand. And he returns to the distant planet. Back and forth he goes. When he transplants all of this planet to that distant planet, it will only be breakfast time in eternity."* We cannot grasp in our finite minds the infinite power and everlasting presence of our Almighty God. What a promise that holds for our hearts—that the God we love was, and is, and forever more will be. Praise His Holy Name!

WHITE SANDS NATIONAL MONUMENT, NEW MEXICO

THE WONDER OF *God* FOR US

THE WONDER OF GOD FOR US

GOD'S SALVATION IN CHRIST

I have chosen you.

DEUTERONOMY 7:6

You are uniquely and divinely created. You are chosen to be a co-heir with the Son of God to the glories and riches of heaven. What a wonderful salvation is yours! Have you ever wondered when you became so special to Him? It was in the counsel halls of eternity. It was before He swung this world into space. You were on His heart before anything was. You are special, like none other. What a humbling thought to know that we were in the heart and the mind of God before the foundation of this world! God is for us!

THE *BLESSING*

In Thy presence is fulness of joy;
in Thy right hand there are pleasures forever.

PSALM 16:11

Nestled in the hills of the Great Smoky Mountains is this quaint country church. With nothing else around and the mist hugging the trees, it would almost appear that this little church is lost. Yet, in Psalm 139, we read that wherever we go, God's presence is there. And in His presence is joy forevermore! Like the mist that shrouds this little church, the Spirit of God is present in the world. What a blessing to know He is always there. And He is calling your name. Job 36:6 says, *"He is wooing you from the jaws of distress to a spacious place free from restriction"* (NIV). Will you answer His call?

GREAT SMOKY MOUNTAINS NATIONAL PARK, TENNESSEE

LIVING *Water*

"If any man is thirsty, let him come to Me and drink . . .

from his innermost being shall flow rivers of living water."

JOHN 7:37,38

Imagine this scene for a moment. You're on a hike and have become lost. Worse yet, you have forgotten your canteen. Hours pass, and finding water is all you care about. Soon you hear the sound of rushing water. You don't hesitate, but run to the source. You've never tasted water this sweet and cool. But here's the rub. You have no way to carry the water with you for the return trip. How will you make it? In John 7, we read about Jesus' response to people celebrating at an annual feast. In the world's eyes they weren't lost—they were having a terrific time. Yet their enjoyment was only temporal. On the last day of the feast, Jesus cried out to the revelers, *"If any man is thirsty, let him come to Me and drink"* (John 7:37, NASB). Jesus is your only way to true and lasting satisfaction. Are you thirsty? Come and drink. The waters are stirring for you today.

GREAT SMOKY MOUNTAINS NATIONAL PARK, TENNESSEE

HEAVEN'S *Window*

For God, who said, "Light shall shine out of darkness,"

is the One who has shone in our hearts

to give the light of the knowledge…of Christ.

II CORINTHIANS 4:6

I have always loved natural science. I can remember when my fourth grade teacher taught me about photosynthesis. I was enthralled by this concept. She said, *"The word* photo *means 'light,' and* synthesis *means 'to put together.'"* If you were to take away our sunlight, this world would become cold, dark, and dead—just like a man without Jesus. When Jesus came into this world, He brought the light of the knowledge of God. Do you want your life put back together? Come to the light of Jesus. Divine photosynthesis occurs when the light of God's Word enters our hearts. Praise God that the light of Christ shines in our hearts to give us knowledge of the infinite mercies and grace of Almighty God. Jesus said, *"I am come that they might have life, and that they might have it more abundantly"* (John 10:10b).

SLOT CANYON, ARIZONA

THE HOPE OF *GLORY*

The mystery which has been hidden from the past ages and generations…
has now been manifested…which is Christ in you, the hope of glory.

COLOSSIANS 1:26,27

What is a rainbow? To scientists, it is a series of concentric arcs formed by a collection of water drops reflecting light from a distant source. To a storybook reader, it is an aerial indicator of a pot of gold. For the Christian, it is a sign of hope and the assurance of God's faithfulness (see Genesis 9:8-17). A number of years ago, a submarine sank deep into the Atlantic Ocean off the coast of Massachusetts. A diver went down and heard someone tapping out a message in Morse code: *"Is there any hope?"* Indeed, that's what this world wants to know. And glory to God, there is! Jesus is our hope—the hope of glory! There is an assurance of salvation made possible by His death, burial, and resurrection for every person who will believe. Salvation is a sure thing. It's not a hope-so; it's a know-so assurance for every child of God!

WIND RIVER RANGE, WYOMING

THE *Tree*

And they killed him by hanging him on a tree,

but God raised him from the dead on the third day…

and whoever lives and believes in [him] will never die.

ACTS 10:39,40   JOHN 11:26

This snow-covered tree is a touching reminder of the tree upon which Jesus Christ died for the salvation of man. Upon a tree for all to see, Jesus *"humbled himself, and became obedient unto death, even the death of the cross"* (Philippians 2:8b). Second Corinthians 5:21 says, *"For he hath made him to be sin for us, who knew no sin; that we might be made the righteousness of God in him."* I believe that if God the Father ever wanted to be lenient on sin, it would have been when His own Son was facing the punishment for our sins. But the truth is, God never has and never will overlook sin. Your sin will either be pardoned in Christ or it will be punished in hell. When you realize that the wrath of God was poured out on Jesus for your sin, you'll never be the same. Praise God for the old rugged cross!

CANYONLANDS NATIONAL PARK, UTAH

THE WASHING OF *REGENERATION*

He saved us, not on the basis of deeds which we have done in righteousness,
but according to His mercy, by the washing of regeneration
and renewing by the Holy Spirit.

TITUS 3:5

When we repent of our sins and believe upon Jesus as our Lord and Savior, He regenerates us by the washing of His blood and renews us by the indwelling of the Holy Spirit. God, in His infinite love, reached down to save us from our wretched state of eternal separation from Him. Our works could never save us (Ephesians 2:8-9). God knew the only way we would be forgiven and enjoy His fellowship again was for Him to sacrifice His one and only Son. Our sins had to be atoned for by the blood of the spotless Lamb (read Revelation 1:5 and 7:14). Some people want to call that old-time religion. I call it one-time regeneration! The sinless Son of God died for sinful sons of men. His righteousness covers our sinfulness and washes us clean. Hallelujah!

GRAND CANYON NATIONAL PARK, ARIZONA

AS *W*HITE AS SNOW

Though your sins are as scarlet,

they will be as white as snow.

ISAIAH 1:18

When you look at the snow on this glacial lake and read this verse from Isaiah, do you say to yourself, *"I can never be that clean. I've done so many horrible things"*? Or do you say, *"Praise God! I am as clean as the new-fallen snow! Even the worst of my sin is washed clean in the blood of my Savior Jesus"*? If you are like the first person in this scenario, I have good news! God is a God of grace. He is a God of forgiveness. And He is a God of the second chance. When you confess your sins, the cleansing tides of Calvary sweep across your soul, and every blot, blur, and blemish that ever stained you is washed whiter than snow in the blood of Jesus. HALLELUJAH! Amen and Amen.

WIND RIVER RANGE, WYOMING

FROM DARKNESS TO *Light*

That you may proclaim the excellencies of Him
who has called you out of darkness into His marvelous light.

I PETER 2:9

Imagine being lost in a cave for hours, even days, and desperately longing to see the light of day or even hear a human voice. You're immobilized with fear. Then without warning, you hear your name and someone shouting, *"Are you there? Come! Come here! I know the way out!"* The next thing you see is a light beam headed your way. Joy, oh joy! Nothing can compare to the outburst of relief you feel. You've been rescued! In the same way, Jesus is calling you out of darkness into His glorious light. If you haven't answered His call, I encourage you to do that right now. Surrender the dark vestiges of your life to the glorious vistas of His light. Flee the darkness and run to the light. The eternal flame of His love will never die.

GRAND CANYON NATIONAL PARK, ARIZONA

A PLACE IN THE *SON*

If any man is in Christ,

he is a new creature: the old things passed away;

behold, new things have come.

II CORINTHIANS 5:17

The unique colors and curves in this rock formation have a special place in the sun, just as each child of God has a special place in the Son—the Body of Christ. You are a new and ever-changing reflection of His glory, just like this rock formation. With each passing day, the winds caress a new curve and the waters carve a new crevice in this rock. And as a child of God, the blood of Christ washes you, and the Holy Spirit breathes new life into you. I challenge you to write down and memorize the following statement written by Robert McGee in his book, Search for Significance: *"I am deeply loved, completely forgiven, fully pleasing, totally accepted, and absolutely complete in Christ."* Believe it, my friend, because you are!

VERMILLION CLIFFS WILDERNESS AREA, ARIZONA

Vision

Looking unto Jesus

the author and finisher of our faith.

The book of Proverbs tells us, *"Where there is no vision, the people perish"* (28:19). Praise God that He had the vision to save mankind from eternal damnation. Glory to Jesus for going before us to prepare the way—and not just to prepare it, but to purchase it by His death. God knew that we couldn't work our way to heaven (Isaiah 64:6). My friend, I wouldn't trust the best fifteen minutes I ever lived to get me to heaven, much less some of my worst minutes. If we could earn our way to heaven, why would God allow His Son to die? What kind of a Father would do that? Praise God that He not only authored your salvation by sending His Son, but He finished your salvation by allowing His Son to die in your place. Oh, the joy that will be ours when we see Him face-to-face!

CANYONLANDS NATIONAL PARK, UTAH

THE *L*IGHT AT THE END OF THE TUNNEL

These things I have written to you

who believe in the name of the Son of God,

in order that you may know that you have eternal life.

I JOHN 5:13

I know that I am saved and am on my way to heaven. Can you say that? If not, let me tell you on the authority of the Word of God that if you repent of your sin and put your trust in Jesus Christ to save you, then you're going to heaven. The Lord Jesus Christ took off His royal robes in heaven, came to earth to be born of a virgin, lived a sinless life, and died upon a cross—pouring out His rich, red, royal blood as an atonement for your sin and to satisfy the righteous demands of a holy God. Jesus said, *"I give unto them eternal life; and they shall never perish, neither shall any man pluck them out of my hand"* (John 10:28). May you know that the light at the end of the tunnel is the light of Jesus Christ!

Zion National Park, Utah

NEITHER *H*EIGHT NOR DEPTH

*N*either height nor depth, nor anything else in all creation,
will be able to separate us from the love of God that is in Christ Jesus our Lord.

ROMANS 8:39

The Colorado River is located 3,000 feet below where Tom was standing when he took this photograph. That's quite a height from where he stood. And quite a depth from which he could fall. I want you to re-read the Scripture that accompanies this powerful photograph. There is nothing in heaven above or hell below that can separate you from the love of God. Nothing—no, nothing—can separate you from His love. Is there anything better than being saved? Yes, there is. It's being saved and knowing that you're saved. Friend, you can know you're saved, not because of what you've done, but because of what Jesus has done. Nothing can separate you from that Love which went to the cross for you and now reigns in heaven for you.

GRAND CANYON NATIONAL PARK, ARIZONA

STANDING *F*IRM

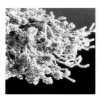

*S*tand firm in the faith. . .

Let all that you do be done in love.

I Corinthians 16:13,14

This snow-covered tree looks like it is anything but "standing firm" on the precipice of the Grand Canyon. But we must remember that standing firm has nothing to do with appearances. Instead, it has everything to do with faith. *"Now faith is the substance of things hoped for, the evidence of things not seen"* (Hebrews 11:1). "Substance" in this passage means solid ground. When we are living by faith, we are standing upon the solid rock of Jesus. And the "evidence of things not seen" is what is already in the heart and mind of God. He sees His children bathed in the light and glory of Jesus who has washed away their sin and made them clean and holy. The door through which Jesus enters your heart—and thereby makes you His temple—swings upon the hinges of grace, and faith is the key that unlocks that door.

GRAND CANYON NATIONAL PARK, ARIZONA

THE *L*IGHT OF THE WORLD

"I am the light of the world;
he who follows Me shall not walk in the darkness, but shall have the light of life."

JOHN 8:12

Light has come into the world. And His name is Jesus. He came into the world to defeat the darkness and shine the glory of God into the hearts of men. Have you ever wondered where the darkness came from? The devil started this battle when he turned against God. He was Lucifer, the "the son of the morning," and he became Satan, "the father of night." Now, let me ask you: Who wins when dark and light compete? Light…always. The dark is absolutely powerless against the light. If you're in a dark room, how do you get the darkness out? With a vacuum cleaner? A broom? No. The only thing that will remove the dark is when you turn on the light. The darkness flees. It cannot stay. It is totally powerless against the light. What a glorious thought! The Light has come into the world. And His name is Jesus.

Peacham, Vermont

THE WONDER OF *GOD* WITH US

GOD'S SUFFICIENCY IN LIFE

I will be with you.

ISAIAH 43:2

Jesus said He would be with you always—even to the end of the age. He didn't qualify this statement with, *"I will be with you sometimes, but not when you walk through the fires of temptation."* Or, *"I will be with you most of the time, but not when you pass through the waters of tribulation."* He said He would be with you always. What a comfort! If you are a child of God, you have the powerful presence of the Holy Spirit residing in you forevermore. Never a day need you feel lonely. Never a day need you feel abandoned. Never alone. We have the wonder of His presence with us always.

MT. NEBO'S *Vista*

The Lord's *lovingkindnesses indeed never cease,*

for His compassions never fail.

They are new every morning; great is Thy faithfulness.

LAMENTATIONS 3:22-23

No matter where we've been or what we've done, we can begin anew because of God's merciful forgiveness. What a way to wake each morning and know His compassions never fail. Now, that's something a sleeping pill will never do! Do you see those still waters in front of Mt. Nebo? Think of that as God's steadfast love for you. Our actions don't disturb the waters of God's love. His love is faithfully unconditional. God does not say, *"I will love you if…"* or *"I will love you when…"*. If God's love for you depended upon anything in you, then if that thing in you changed, God's love toward you would change. Second Timothy 2:13a tells us, however, that even *"If we are faithless, He remains faithful"* (NASB). The God who saved you is the God who will keep you.

SAN JUAN MOUNTAINS, COLORADO

THE *W*ATCHMAN OF ZION

Unless the LORD *builds the house, they labor in vain who build it;*
unless the LORD *guards the city, the watchman keeps awake in vain.*

PSALM 127:1

If only we knew how dependent we are upon our great Watchman—God Himself. We think we're in charge—going hither and yonder, doing this and that. And all the while, God sees our finite ways. He notes our prideful steps yet never leaves us. He is our Watchman who never sleeps. He is our Provider who knows our needs. If you will surrender completely to Him, you will never be disappointed. He will be your everything. When you build your life upon the Rock, you will have the firm assurance of Matthew 7:24-25: *"Therefore whosoever heareth these sayings of mine, and doeth them, I will liken him unto a wise man, which built his house upon a rock: And the rain descended, and the floods came, and the winds blew, and beat upon that house; and it fell not: for it was founded upon a rock."* And that Rock is Jesus—the Rock of Ages.

ZION NATIONAL PARK, UTAH

FIELD OF *Dreams*

"Observe how the [flowers] of the field grow....
If God so arrays the grass of the field...will He not much more do so for you?"

MATTHEW 6:28,30

If you've fussed and fumed through life's challenges, wondering if the Sovereign Creator was napping under a shade tree, I have a message for you: God is still on the throne and He is still watching over you. The God who hung the stars, poured the oceans, and raised the mountains is still here. Look at the flowers in this field. Your loving Father has dressed this hillside with beauty. He will do the same for you. Perhaps you've made Jesus the Savior of your life but have never allowed Him to be the Lord of your life through your darkest hours and most difficult days. You can do that today by asking His forgiveness and surrendering to Him: *"Casting all your care upon him; for he careth for you"* (1 Peter 5:7). He cares. He truly does.

WIND RIVER RANGE, WYOMING

IN THE *MIDST* OF THE STORM

It is good for me that I was afflicted;

that I may learn thy statutes.

PSALM 119:71

Did the psalmist really say, *"It is good for me that I have been afflicted"*? Yes, as hard as it seems, that's what he said. And for good reason. He knew that a higher purpose would be accomplished. You see, just a few verses before this one, the psalmist said, *"Before I was afflicted I went astray, but now I have kept thy word"* (Psalm 119:67). There was a progression to the psalmist's revelation. He went astray. He became afflicted. But then he acknowledged the power of God's Word to see him through his afflictions. Faith, like film, is best developed in the darkness. Think back on your own life. When did you learn the greatest lessons? In the light of good times? Or in the darkness of bad times? If you will yield all of you to all of Him, indeed you'll agree that it is good for you to be afflicted so you may draw closer to God and learn from Him.

GRAND CANYON NATIONAL PARK, ARIZONA

THE *VALLEY* OF THE SHADOW OF DEATH

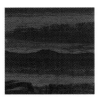

Even though I walk through the valley of the shadow of death,

I fear no evil; for Thou art with me.

PSALM 23:4

We are living on the very precipice of eternity. You and I are in the shadow of death every day. Whether we know it or not, like it or not, accept it or not, death is a prevailing matter. Just over the other side of right now is eternity. Where do you stand? My friend, are you trusting in Jesus to hold your hand through eternity? God has prepared the way through the valley; it is not a place of permanence, but a place of passage. He knows every twist and turn, every changing shadow, every den where danger lurks. God is with you! When you pass through the valley of the shadow of death, His power will be there with you to sustain you. His rod will protect you from the powers of evil, and His staff will draw you close to Him.

CANYONLANDS NATIONAL PARK, UTAH

JOY IN THE MORNING

Weeping may last for the night,

but a shout of joy comes in the morning.

PSALM 30:5

I lived through many a storm during my childhood in Florida. And one thing I can say with certainty—God always brings a calm after a storm. Though the night may be torn apart by gale force winds, crackling peals of thunder, and blinding flashes of lightning, the sun will blaze through the clearing clouds on the horizon the next morning. I see such a thing in this poignant sunrise at Tennessee's Reelfoot Lake. It's as though God's power has burst through the darkness and given us new hope and renewed joy. The calm has once again returned. His peace has robbed the night of its despair. Oh, that we might trust God's Word when He promises that joy will follow weeping. My friend, you can rest assured that if you go to bed despondent and hopeless, His joy will come in the morning.

Reelfoot Lake State Park, Tennessee

*P*EACE, BE STILL

*P*eace, be still.

MARK 4:39

What do you see when you look at this image from the middle of winter at Yellowstone National Park? At first glance, I see perfect peace. Though as I look closer, I notice that a fire blazed through this thicket of trees months before. Isn't that how it is with us? At first glance, most people just see the peace that Jesus brings to our lives, but they don't know about the fires out of which our peace was born. The purity of His peace comes and washes us clean— almost as if the fire had never singed our garments of faith. God's presence empowers us to face the fires, then His peace enlivens us when the fires go out. What do people see when they meet you? The charred remains of a restless heart? Or God's peacefulness in an abiding heart?

Yellowstone National Park, Wyoming

A WELLSPRING OF *HOPE*

"For I know the plans that I have for you," declares the LORD,

"plans for welfare and not for calamity

to give you a future and a hope."

JEREMIAH 29:11

I don't know what your future holds. But I can tell you, on the authority of the Word of God, that He has a wonderful plan for you. Some find that hard to believe because they're afraid if they let go of their agenda, God may send them off to a remote jungle or call them to a life of singleness. Friend, God's plan will be the best thing that has ever happened to you! His thoughts are higher than our thoughts. We cannot in our wildest imaginations know what is best for ourselves. But we can know that the Creator of all things can do what is best for us. A wellspring of hope will bubble up inside you when you realize the awesome love your Father has for you. He's just waiting for you to step down off the throne and make Him Lord of your life.

Great Smoky Mountains National Park, Tennessee

QUIET TIME

In the early morning, while it was still dark, He arose…
and departed to a lonely place, and was praying there.

MARK 1:35

People in the Christian community talk often about having a "quiet time." Well, what is a quiet time? Think of it as a daily date with God. Think back to your first date. Would you ever have considered it simply an item on your "to do" list? That's absurd. You anticipated that date with excitement—longing for the day and the hour to arrive. Can you imagine having that kind of thrill each morning when you get alone with God? Psalm 63:1 says, *"O God, thou art my God; early will I seek thee: my soul thirsteth for thee, my flesh longeth for thee in a dry and thirsty land, where no water is."* That's the heart of our Savior when He went off to pray. His secret place of solitude became a sacred place of communion.

WIND RIVER RANGE, WYOMING

REFLECTED *Glory*

As in water face reflects face,

so the heart of man reflects man.

PROVERBS 27:19

Have you ever wondered what your purpose is in life? To reflect God's glory. You are created in God's image to be a reflection of Christ's likeness. He formed you out of dust and breathed eternal life into your soul. You are His masterpiece—the handiwork of a loving Father. Are you bearing that family likeness today? When someone looks at your life, do they see you, or do they see Jesus? Now, I am a Rogers. My father's name was Arden Duncan Rogers, and I am a partaker of his nature. You would expect to find some of his physical traits and character qualities in me because he fathered me. In the same way, you are a child of God. He has created you in His image and has called you to be a reflection of His glory. Could there be any greater calling on your life than to reflect the Savior to a lost world?

WIND RIVER RANGE, WYOMING

GREAT IS THY *F*AITHFULNESS

*A*nd let us consider how to stimulate one another to love and good deeds,

not forsaking our own assembling together…but encouraging one another;

and all the more, as you see the day drawing near.

HEBREWS 10:24,25

Faithfulness is a quality all of us admire. First Corinthians 4:2 says, *"Moreover it is required in stewards, that a man be found faithful."* What do I mean by faithfulness? Integrity, honesty, trustworthiness, and loyalty. Are you someone others can count upon? One of the surest marks of faithfulness in Christians is their faithfulness to the local Body of Christ. Look around you. Are the days in which we live so filled with godliness that we think we can forsake the assembling of ourselves? We owe it to one another as members of the Body of Christ to be loyal and faithful. We need each other. When you come to church, you're saying, *"You're important"* to the pastor, to the person sitting next to you, and most importantly to God. Will you say, *"Today, I will be faithful to the faith. I will be faithful to the fight. I will be faithful to the finish"*?

GREAT SMOKY MOUNTAINS NATIONAL PARK, TENNESSEE

ENTER BY THE *NARROW* GATE

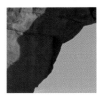

"Enter by the narrow gate; for the gate is wide,
and the way is broad that leads to destruction . . .
For the gate is small, and the way is narrow that leads to life."

MATTHEW 7:13,14

Every path is going somewhere. In fact, the path you're on right now is headed somewhere. Let me ask you, *"When you get to where you're going, where will you be?"* You have the greatest of privileges—it's called a free will. God, in His infinite wisdom, gave each of us the opportunity to map out our journey choice by choice. You are free to choose, but you are not free not to choose; you are not free to choose the consequence of your choice. Knowing this, you must choose your path wisely, for it will determine your destiny. And praise Jesus, He has walked the way before and has promised to guide you. *"Trust in the LORD with all thine heart; and lean not unto thine own understanding. In all thy ways acknowledge him, and he shall direct thy paths"* (Proverbs 3:5-6).

ARCHES NATIONAL PARK, UTAH

FIRMLY PLANTED

And he will be like a tree firmly planted by streams of water,

which yields its fruit in its season, and its leaf does not wither;

and in whatever he does, he prospers.

PSALM 1:3

One of the most unqualified promises in the Bible is found in the first chapter of the Psalms. The psalmist compares a righteous man to a tree firmly planted by streams of water. He says that whatever this man does, he shall prosper. Immediately, most people interpret that as wealth. But God does not guarantee material wealth. God's definition of prosperity means that we will enjoy an abundant life where He meets the needs for our general welfare. Do you want to know the key to prosperity? It is found in the preceding verse: *"But his delight is in the law of the LORD, and in His law he meditates day and night"* (Psalm 1:2, NASB). Plant yourself firmly in the Word of God, follow Him with all your heart, and He will provide for you. He will prosper you.

ESCALANTE WILDERNESS AREA, UTAH

*S*TEADFAST

Therefore, my beloved brethren,

be steadfast, immovable, always abounding in the work of the Lord,

knowing that your toil is not in vain in the Lord.

I CORINTHIANS 15:58

One of the greatest examples of steadfast faith is found in the story of Shadrach, Meshach, and Abed-Nego, who refused to bow to the golden image of King Nebuchadnezzar. They said, *"Our God whom we serve is able to deliver us from the burning fiery furnace, and he will deliver us out of thine hand, O king. But if not, be it known unto thee, O king, that we will not serve thy gods, nor worship the golden image which thou hast set up"* (Daniel 3:17-18). It's one thing to have faith to escape. But it's another thing to have faith to endure. That takes steadfast faith. Our God is able to deliver us; but if He doesn't deliver us, it's not because He can't. God may not always deliver you from your tribulations and temptations. But He will give you faith to be steadfast, so that you can be always abounding in the work He gives you.

White Sands National Monument, New Mexico

HE IS COMING

Behold, He is coming with the clouds;

and every eye will see Him.

REVELATION 1:7

When Jesus came the first time, He came in a manger. When He comes again, He is coming in majesty. The first time, He shed His royal blood for our redemption. When He comes again, He is going to be dressed in royal robes to reign in righteousness. The first time, He came to a crucifixion. When He comes again, He is coming to a coronation. No longer will He wear a crown of thorns, but He will wear a diadem of glory. The first time He came, He was despised and rejected of men. When He comes again, every knee will bow. The clouds will be resplendent in glory as He triumphantly steps out of heaven. And we will meet Him face to face. HALLELUJAH—it may be sooner than we think!

WIND RIVER RANGE, WYOMING

ANCIENT OF *DAYS*

"I am the Alpha and the Omega,
the first and the last, the beginning and the end."

REVELATION 22:13

Within this canyon portal are the ancient remains of an Indian civilization. It's just a glimmer of the eternal perspective of our God whose name is "I AM." Did you notice that this name God gave Himself is an incomplete sentence? Now, most people would finish that sentence, *"I am…(something)"* But not our Lord. He purposefully did not complete the sentence, because He is all we will ever need. Are you hungry? He is the bread. Are you in the dark? He is the light. Are you searching? He is the truth. Are you lost? He is the way. He is the "I AM." He is the beginning and the end. To God be the glory, for He is THE *W*ONDER OF IT ALL.

CANYONLANDS NATIONAL PARK, UTAH

PHOTOGRAPHER'S ACKNOWLEDGMENTS

He hideth my soul in the cleft of the rock
That shadows a dry, thirsty land.
He hideth my life in the depths of his love,
And covers me there with His hand.
- Fanny J. Crosby

I am deeply indebted to many people for their help and encouragement in making this book—this dream—a reality. Over the years many friends have traveled with me as I have pursued the art of photography; for your support and fellowship, I am so grateful. My friends Dave Perdue and his assistant Sharon Gardner have not only provided invaluable administrative help, but more importantly, they have believed in me. The staff at *Love Worth Finding Ministries*, Bill Skelton, Cathy Allen, and Julia Flanagan, have worked enthusiastically to make this book possible; Julia deserves special credit for her diligent and insightful editorial skill. Furthermore, Ricky King, Lawrence Kimbrough, Diana Lawrence, and the staff at Broadman and Holman Publishers have been a joy to work with; Diana Lawrence deserves further acknowledgment for her inspired creativity and attention to detail in designing this book. I want to thank all of you.

Finally, for several years I have had the pleasure and priviledge of studying and learning from my pastor, Adrian Rogers. His steadfast devotion and loving example have been such an inspiration for me . . . to exemplify the beauty of the Creator's works and to encourage all of us to walk in His ways.

Tom Fox

AUTHOR'S ACKNOWLEDGMENTS

From the moment I saw the photography of Tom Fox, I knew that God had anointed this young man with a gift that few possess. And that gift is to show the world the beauty, the power and the majesty of Almighty God. I am thankful for the opportunity I had to write my reflections of these beautiful images.

I also wish to thank my dear wife, Joyce, who through the years has been a companion to me and side by side has enjoyed the sights and sounds of God's creation. How often we have taken walks and in awesome wonder discussed the beauty of God's creation.

I am grateful, as well, for George Beverly Shea who penned the words and music behind the title of this book. His love for God is an inspiration to me and others who through the years have enjoyed his rich, baritone voice and ministry through the Billy Graham Association.

The people of Broadman and Holman have been a supportive group of friends and associates for years, and it was with great pleasure that I was afforded another opportunity to produce a book with these servants of the Lord.

Words are inadequate to express my profound gratitude for the giftedness and willing spirit of my editorial assistant Julia Flanagan. It is her special touch that sometimes transforms my words into a better form and style without distorting my heartbeat.

Finally, I am most grateful to God that He has allowed me the greatest of gifts to be engrafted into His vine and given the privilege of telling the world about Jesus—the greatest Love worth finding. It is my prayer that if you have never met the God Who gave His Son to die for you, that this book will lead you into the way of life everlasting as His child. And if you have met the Savior, that this book will deepen your resolve to love Him more with each day He gives you.

Adrian Rogers